Twenty to Make
Knitted Egg Cosies

Susie Johns

Search Press

First published in Great Britain 2011
Search Press Limited
Wellwood, North Farm Road,
Tunbridge Wells, Kent TN2 3DR

Text copyright © Susie Johns 2011

Photographs by Paul Bricknell at
Search Press Studios

Photographs and design copyright
© Search Press Ltd 2011

ISBN: 978-1-84448-634-2

Suppliers
If you have difficulty in obtaining any of the
materials and equipment mentioned in this book,
then please visit the Search Press website for
details of suppliers: www.searchpress.com

Printed in Malaysia

Dedication
For my wonderful children:
Josh, Lillie and Edith.

Contents

Introduction

These knitted egg cosies are fun to make and a great way to use up oddments of yarn. 'Novelty' knits make good gifts: a bride and groom as a wedding present, perhaps; a pumpkin for Halloween; a rabbit for Easter; a penguin, snowman or Christmas pudding as a stocking filler; plain or striped cosies for a housewarming gift; or any of the others for birthdays, anniversaries or other special occasions. Many of the projects could even double up as finger puppets, making them ideal for children – as long as you sew the components together very securely.

Because most of the projects are small, they are relatively quick to knit, though you should allow extra time for the making up and sewing in of yarn ends. Most of the patterns are designed to be knitted in the round on a set of four double-pointed needles. For components to be knitted back and forth in rows, instead of using regular knitting needles you could just use two of the double-pointed needles, if you find this easier.

Make family breakfasts fun with the help of some hand-knitted egg cosies. Here is a selection of the designs featured in this book.

Materials and techniques

Knitting on four needles can be tricky, especially when you are working the first few rows. To cast on, use the two-needle method, sometimes called 'chain' cast-on, as it will create a firm, tight edge that is less likely to slip off the needles. For most of the patterns, you will see that the first row (or round) is knitted by inserting the needle into the back loop of each stitch, which also helps to form a firm edge.

The needle sizes given in the patterns are smaller than you might expect and you may have to use a larger or smaller needle size than the one recommended in order to produce a firm, close-knit fabric that will hold its shape and not allow any stuffing to poke through.

The projects are mostly made from double knitting yarn, though some of the smaller items use 4-ply. As a general rule, I prefer to use natural fibres in my knitting projects, particularly pure wool, as it has a natural elasticity. In some cases, though, I have had to use acrylic yarns and various blends in order to source suitable colours. For the main colours in each project, quantities are stated in balls but you will not use a whole ball, so before you go shopping for yarns, experiment with any oddments you already have. If you need to buy only a small amount of a certain colour, tapestry yarns are a good choice as they are similar in thickness to double knitting, are sold in small skeins and are available in a wider choice of colours than most knitting yarns.

Tension guide

Most of the patterns in this book are knitted to a similar tension – 12 sts and 18 rows to 10cm (4in), measured over stocking stitch on 2.75mm (UK 12; US 2) needles, using DK yarn.

To be sure that your tension matches, work a swatch using spare DK yarn on 2.75mm (UK 12; US 2) needles and measure it. If you have more stitches over 10cm (4in), this indicates that you knit more tightly than the stated tension (or gauge) and your egg cosy is likely to end up smaller than the one in the picture, so use a larger needle; if you have fewer stitches, this means that you tend to knit more loosely, so choose a smaller needle.

Abbreviations

st(s)	stitch(es)
k	knit
p	purl
SS	stocking stitch
sl	slip
psso	pass slip stitch over
rep	repeat
rem	remaining
inc	increase
inc1	knit into front and back of same stitch*
inc2	knit into front, back and front of stitch**
dec	decrease
RS	right side
WS	wrong side
tbl	through back loop(s)
k2tog	knit 2 together
k2tog tbl	knit 2 together through back loops
yfwd	yarn forward
beg	begin(ning)
DK	double knitting

*Where the pattern states 'inc1', knit into the front and back of the stitch, thereby creating one extra stitch.

**Where the pattern states 'inc2', knit into the front, the back and the front again, thereby creating two extra stitches.

These colourful cosies can be found on pages 42–43. Knitted using the same basic pattern, only the colours used and the detailing have been changed. With a little bit of imagination and knitting know-how, all the patterns in this book can be adapted to make a personalised gift for a special friend or relative.

Retro Stripes

Materials:

2 balls DK yarn (wool or wool blend) – white and turquoise

small amount of DK yarn (wool or wool blend) – red

Needles:

set of four 2.75mm (UK 12; US 2) double-pointed knitting needles

tapestry needle

Instructions:

With set of four 2.75mm (UK 12; US 2) double-pointed needles and turquoise DK yarn, cast on 36 sts and distribute between three needles.
Round 1: k each st tbl.
Rounds 2 and 3: join in white DK yarn and k.
Rounds 4–18: knit a further 15 rounds, changing colour after every 2 rounds, to create striped pattern.
Cut white yarn and continue in turquoise.
Round 19: (k4, k2tog) six times [30 sts].
Round 20: k.
Round 21: (k3, k2tog) six times [24 sts].
Round 22: k.
Round 23: (k2, k2tog) six times [18 sts].
Cut yarn and thread through rem 6 sts.

Cord

With two 2.75mm (UK 12; US 2) double-pointed needles and red DK yarn, cast on 2 sts.
Rows 1–60: k2; do not turn but slide sts to other end of needle.
Cut yarn, leaving a tail for sewing up, and fasten off.

Making up

Pull up the yarn at the top of the egg cosy to gather; fasten off. Fold the cord to create four loops and stitch to the top of the cosy.

Stripes for Breakfast

Use three colours of yarn instead of two – red, white and blue – for a patriotic version of this simple egg cosy. These egg cosies are 6cm (2¼in) high (excluding loops).

Early Birds

Materials:

1 ball DK yarn (wool or wool blend) –
   pale yellow

small scraps of wool felt – red and yellow

2 small glass beads – black

sewing thread – red and black

Needles:

set of four 2.75mm (UK 12; US 2) double-
   pointed knitting needles

tapestry needle

sewing needle

Instructions:

Body and head (worked in one piece)

With set of four 2.75mm (UK 12; US 2) double-
pointed needles and pale yellow DK yarn, cast
on 36 sts and distribute between three needles.
Round 1: k each st tbl.
Rounds 2–21: k.
Round 22: (k4, k2tog) six times [30 sts].
Round 23: k.
Round 24: (k3, k2tog) six times [24 sts].

Round 25: k.
Round 26: (k2, k2tog) six times [18 sts].
Round 27: k.
Round 28: (k1, k2tog) six times [12 sts].
Rounds 29–33: k.
Round 34: (k3, inc1) three times [15 sts].
Rounds 35–37: k.
Round 38: (k3, k2tog) three times [12 sts].
Round 39: (k2, k2tog) three times [9 sts].
Round 40: (k1, k2tog) three times [6 sts].
Round 41: k2tog three times.
Cut yarn and thread through rem 3 sts.

Wing (make 2)

With two 2.75mm (UK 12; US 2) needles and
pale yellow DK yarn, cast on 3 sts.
Row 1: k each st tbl.
Row 2: p.
Row 3: inc1, k1, inc1 [5 sts].
Row 4: p.
Row 5: inc1, k3, inc1 [7 sts].
Rows 6–12: beg with a p row, work 7 rows in SS.
Row 13: k1, sl1, k1, psso, k1, k2tog, k1 [5 sts].
Row 14: p.
Row 15: k1, sl1, k2tog, psso, k1 [3 sts].
Row 16: p.
Row 17: sl1, k2tog, psso; cut yarn and
fasten off.

Making up

Flatten the egg cosy. Stitch the wings in place,
on the front and the back. Cut a comb and
beak from red felt and stitch them in place. Cut
two small circles of yellow felt for the eyes, then
stitch a black bead in the centre of each, taking
the needle and thread right through the head
to help maintain the flattened shape.

Gone Quackers!

For a duck, use white yarn and cut a bill from yellow felt. The height of these egg cosies is 10cm (4in).

Pink and Perky

Materials:

1 ball DK yarn (wool or wool blend) – pink
polyester fibrefill
2 small glass beads – black
black thread

Needles:

set of four 2.75mm (UK 12; US 2) double-
    pointed knitting needles
tapestry needle
sewing needle

Instructions:

Body and head (worked in one piece)

With set of four 2.75mm (UK 12; US 2) double-
pointed needles and pink yarn, cast on 36 sts
and distribute between three needles.
Round 1: k each st tbl.
Rounds 2–25: k.
Round 26: (k4, k2tog) six times [30 sts].
Round 27: k.
Round 28: (k3, k2tog) six times [24 sts].
Round 29: (k2, k2tog) six times [18 sts].
Round 30: (k1, k2tog) six times [12 sts].
Round 31: k2tog six times [6 sts].
Round 32: inc1 in each st [12 sts].
Round 33: (k1, inc1) six times [18 sts].
Round 34: (k2, inc1) six times [24 sts].
Round 35: (k3, inc1) six times [30 sts].
Rounds 36–44: k.
Round 45: (k3, k2tog) six times [24 sts].
Round 46: k.
Rounds 47–49: as rounds 29–31.
Cut yarn, leaving a tail for sewing up, and
thread through rem 6 sts.

Trotters (make 2)

With two 2.75mm (UK 12; US 2) needles and
pink yarn, cast on 3 sts.
Row 1: inc1 in each st [6 sts].
Row 2: p.
Row 3: inc1 in each st [12 sts].
Rows 4–14: beg with a p row, work 11 rows
in SS.

Row 15: k1, sl1, psso, k6, k2tog, k1 [10 sts].
Row 16 and each even-numbered (RS) row: p.
Row 17: k1, sl1, psso, k4, k2tog, k1 [8 sts].
Row 19: k1, sl1, psso, k2, k2tog, k1 [6 sts].
Row 21: k1, sl1, psso, k2tog, k1 [4 sts].
Row 23: k1, k2tog, k1 [3 sts].
Row 25: sl1, k2tog, psso; cut yarn and fasten off.

Snout

With two 2.75mm (UK 12; US 2) needles and
pink yarn, cast on 4 sts.
Rows 1–48: sl1, k3.
Cast off.

Ears (make 2)

With two 2.75mm (UK 12; US 2) needles and
pink yarn, cast on 11 sts.
Row 1: k each st tbl.
Row 2: k4, sl1, k2tog, psso, k4 [9 sts].
Rows 3, 5, 7 and 9: k.
Row 4: k3, sl1, k2tog, psso, k3 [7 sts].
Row 6: k2, sl1, k2tog, psso, k2 [5 sts].
Row 8: k1, sl1, k2tog, psso, k1 [3 sts].
Row 10: sl1, k2tog, psso [1 st].
Cut yarn, leaving a tail for sewing up, and
fasten off.

Tail

With two 2.75mm (UK 12; US 2) needles and
pink yarn, cast on 10 sts.
Row 1: inc1 in each st [20 sts], then cast off.

Making up

Pull up the yarn end at the top of the head and fasten off. Stuff the head with polyester fibrefill. Run a gathering thread around the neckline and pull up slightly. Stitch the seams on the trotters then stitch the sloping edges to the sides of the body. Roll up the snout into a tight spiral and stitch it in place. Thread the yarn through the cast-on edge of each ear and pull up slightly, then stitch each ear to the head. Stitch the tail in place. Sew on the two black beads for eyes, using black sewing thread.

Get the day off to a good start with a delicious boiled egg. The piggy egg cosy measures 11cm (4¼in) in height.

Easter Bunny

Materials:

1 ball Aran yarn (wool or wool blend) – grey

small amounts of DK yarn (wool or wool blend) – pink, orange, green and white

polyester fibrefill

2 sew-on googly eyes

sewing thread – grey or black

Needles:

set of four 3.25mm (UK 10; US 3) double-pointed knitting needles

pair of 3.00mm (UK 11; US 2) knitting needles

tapestry needle

sewing needle

Instructions:

Body and head (work in one piece)

With set of four 3.25mm (UK 10; US 3) double-pointed needles and grey yarn, cast on 30 sts and distribute between three needles.
Round 1: k each st tbl.
Rounds 2–20: k.
Round 21: (k3, k2tog) six times [24 sts].
Round 22: k.
Round 23: (k2, k2tog) six times [18 sts].
Round 24: (k1, k2tog) six times [12 sts].
Round 25: k2tog six times [6 sts].
Round 26: inc1 in each st [12 sts].
Round 27: (k1, inc1) six times [18 sts].
Round 28: (k2, inc1) six times [24 sts].
Round 29: (k3, inc1) six times [30 sts].
Rounds 30–34: k.
Round 35: (k3, k2tog) six times [24 sts].
Round 36: k.
Round 37: (k2, k2tog) six times [18 sts].
Round 38: (k1, k2tog) six times [12 sts].
Round 39: k2tog six times.
Cut yarn and thread through rem 6 sts.

Paws (make 2)

With two 3.25mm (UK 10; US 3) knitting needles and grey yarn, cast on 3 sts.
Row 1: inc1 in each st [6 sts].
Row 2: p.
Row 3: inc1 in each st [12 sts].
Rows 4–14: beg with a p row, work 11 rows of SS.
Row 15: k2tog, k8, k2tog [10 sts].
Row 16: p.
Row 17: k2tog, k6, k2tog [8 sts].
Row 18: p.
Row 19: k2tog, k4, k2tog [6 sts].
Row 20: p2tog, p2, p2tog.
Cast off rem 4 sts.

Ears (make 2)

With two 3.25mm (UK 10; US 3) knitting needles and grey yarn, cast on 3 sts.
Row 1: k all sts tbl.
Rows 2, 4 and 6: p.
Row 3: inc1, k1, inc1 [5 sts].
Row 5: inc1, k3, inc1 [7 sts].
Row 7: inc1, k5, inc1 [9 sts].
Beg with a p row, work 7 rows in SS, then cut yarn and thread through all sts.

Ear lining (make 2)

With 3.00mm (UK 11; US 2) knitting needles and pink DK yarn, cast on 10 sts.
Knit 2 rows, then cast off.

Carrot

Using orange yarn, follow instructions for penguin beak (page 21).

Making up

Stuff the head with polyester fibrefill. Sew the side seams of each paw, then stitch to the sides of the body. Fold the edges of each ear into the centre and oversew them together. Stitch the lining vertically on each ear, then stitch the ears to the head. Sew on the googly eyes. Embroider the nose using pink yarn. Attach a few strands of green yarn to the top of the carrot and fray. Make a small bobble tail from white yarn (see page 30) and stitch it in place.

Teddy Brek

For a teddy, use a bouclé yarn of a similar weight. To make the ears, cast on 2 sts and proceed as follows: Row 1: inc1 in each st [4 sts]. Row 2: k. Row 3: inc1, k2, inc1 [6 sts]. Knit 10 rows. Row 14: k2tog, k2, k2tog [4 sts]. Row 15: k2tog twice [2 sts]; cast off. Fold the ear in half and oversew the edges. For the ear lining, cast on 5 sts using pink yarn and knit 10 rows, then cast off. Stitch the linings to the ears, tucking in the corners to make a smooth, rounded shape. Stitch the ears in place. Embroider the eyebrows and a mouth using black yarn and finish by tying a ribbon bow around the neck. Both egg cosies are about 15cm (6in) high.

Coiled Eggs

Materials:

1 ball 4-ply yarn (wool or wool blend) –
  pale blue

Needles:

set of four 2.25mm (UK 13; US 1) double-
  pointed knitting needles

tapestry needle

Instructions:

With set of four 2.25mm (UK 13; US 1) double-
pointed needles and pale blue yarn, cast on 42
sts and distribute between three needles.
Round 1: k all sts tbl.
Rounds 2–19: k.
Round 20: (k5, k2tog) six times [36 sts].
Round 21 and each odd-numbered round: k.
Round 22: (k4, k2tog) six times [30 sts].
Round 24: (k3, k2tog) six times [24 sts].
Round 26: (k2, k2tog) six times [18 sts].
Round 28: (k1, k2tog) six times [12 sts].
Round 30: k2tog six times [6 sts].

Round 32: k2tog three times [3 sts].
Row 33: k3, do not turn but slide sts to other
end of needle.
Continue using only two needles; rep last row
40 times, then cut yarn and fasten off.

Making up

Coil the cord at the top of the egg cosy into
a neat spiral, catching it into place with a few
discreet stitches.

Flowery Twist

*Make the alternative egg
cosy in exactly the same way
but with navy blue yarn – or
a colour of your choice – and
decorate the top by stitching
a pretty button in the centre of
the spiral on each side. These
cosies measure 10cm (4in) high.*

Snowy Morning

Materials:

1 ball DK fluffy acrylic yarn – bright white
small amounts of 4-ply yarn – red, navy
small amounts of DK yarn – brown, tan, orange
polyester fibrefill
5 tiny pompons – black
black thread

Needles:

set of four 2.75mm (UK 12; US 2) double-
  pointed knitting needles
pair of 2.25mm (UK 13; US 1) knitting needles
tapestry needle
sewing needle

Instructions:

Body and head (worked in one piece)

With set of four 2.75mm (UK 12; US 2) double-
pointed needles and white yarn, cast on 36 sts
and distribute between three needles.
Round 1: k each st tbl.
Rounds 2–25: k.
Round 26: (k4, k2tog) six times [30 sts].
Round 27: k.

Round 28: (k3, k2tog) six times [24 sts].
Round 29: (k2, k2tog) six times [18 sts].
Round 30: (k1, k2tog) six times [12 sts].
Round 31: k2tog six times [6 sts].
Round 32: inc1 in each st [12 sts].
Round 33: (k1, inc1) six times [18 sts].
Round 34: (k2, inc1) six times [24 sts].
Round 35: (k3, inc1) six times [30 sts].
Rounds 36–44: k.
Round 45: (k3, k2tog) six times [24 sts].
Round 46: k.
Rounds 47–49: as rounds 29–31.
Cut yarn, leaving a tail for sewing up, and
thread through rem 6 sts.

Broomstick

With two 2.75mm (UK 12; US 2) needles and
brown DK yarn, cast on 18 sts.
Beg with a k row, work 3 rows in SS.
Cast off purlwise.

Carrot nose

With two 2.75mm (UK 12; US 2) needles and
orange DK yarn, cast on 6 sts.
Rows 1, 3, 5 and 7: k.
Row 2: p5; turn.
Row 4: p4; turn.
Row 6: p3; turn.
Cast off purlwise.

Hat

With set of four 2.75mm (UK 12; US 2) double-
pointed needles and brown DK yarn, cast on
3 sts and distribute evenly between
three needles.
Round 1: inc1 in each st [6 sts].
Round 2: inc1 in each st [12 sts].
Round 3: (k1, inc1) six times [18 sts].
Round 4: (k2, inc1) six times [24 sts].
Round 5: (k3, inc1) six times [30 sts].
Rounds 6–14: k.
Round 15: (k4, inc1) six times [36 sts].
Round 16: (k5, inc1) six times [42 sts].
Round 17: (k6, inc1) six times [48 sts].
Round 18: (k7, inc1) six times [60 sts].
Cast off.

Scarf

With 2.25mm (UK 13; US 1) knitting needles and red 4-ply yarn, cast on 7 sts.
Row 1: k2, (p1, k1) twice, k1.
Row 2: k1, (p1, k1) three times.
Join in navy yarn and rep rows 1 and 2.
Continue repeating these two rows, alternating red and navy yarns to form stripes, until scarf measures approx. 22cm (8¾in); cast off ribwise.

Making up

Stuff the head with polyester fibrefill. Stitch the hat in place. Roll up the carrot nose and stitch in place. Wrap the scarf around the neck and secure with a few stitches. Stitch on pompons for eyes and buttons using black sewing thread. Secure the broomstick by binding it to the body with white yarn. Tie a bundle of tan DK yarn to the top of the broomstick and trim with scissors.

Even the most excited child might be tempted to sit at the breakfast table on Christmas morning by this jolly snowman. He measures 12cm (4¾in) high.

19

Polar Eggsplorer

Materials:

2 balls DK yarn (wool, wool blend or acrylic) –
white and black

small amounts of DK yarn (wool, wool blend or
acrylic) – yellow and orange

polyester fibrefill

2 sew-on googly eyes

Needles:

pair of 2.75mm (UK 12; US 2) knitting needles

tapestry needle

Instructions:

Body (in 2 pieces)

With 2.75mm (UK 12; US 2) needles and white
yarn, cast on 12 sts.
Row 1: k each st tbl.
Row 2: k.
Rows 3–22: beg with a k row, work 20 rows
in SS.
Row 23: k2, k2tog, k4, k2tog tbl, k2 [10 sts].
Row 24: p.
Row 25: k2, k2tog, k2, k2tog tbl, k2 [8 sts].
Row 26: p2, p2tog tbl, p2tog, p2 [6 sts].
Cast off.
With 2.75mm (UK 12; US 2) needles and black
yarn, cast on 24 sts.
Row 1: k each st tbl.
Rows 2 and 3: k.
Row 4: k2, p16, k2.
Rows 5–22: rep rows 3 and 4 nine times.
Row 23: k2, (k2tog, k4) three times, k2tog, k2
[20 sts].
Row 24: k2, p16, k2.
Row 25: k3, (k2tog, k2) three times, k2tog, k3
[16 sts].
Row 26: p2tog eight times [8 sts].
Cast off.

Head (in 2 pieces)

With 2.75mm (UK 12; US 2) needles and white
yarn, cast on 3 sts.
Row 1: p.

Row 2: inc1, k1, inc1 [5 sts].
Row 3: p.
Row 4: inc1, k3, inc1 [7 sts].
Rows 5–15: beg with a p row, work 11 rows
in SS.
Row 16: k1, k2tog, k1, k2tog tbl, k1 [5 sts].
Cast off purlwise.
With 2.75mm (UK 12; US 2) needles and black
yarn, cast on 7 sts.
Row 1: inc1 in each st [14 sts].
Rows 2–19: beg with a p row, work 18 rows
in SS.
Row 20: p2tog seven times.
Cut yarn and thread through rem 7 sts.

Wings (make 2)

With 2.75mm (UK 12; US 2) needles and black
yarn, cast on 10 sts.
Rows 1–8: beg with a k row, work 8 rows in SS.
Row 9: k2tog, k6, k2tog [8 sts].
Rows 10–12: beg with a p row, work 3 rows
in SS.
Row 13: k2tog, k4, k2tog [6 sts].
Rows 14–16: beg with a p row, work 3 rows
in SS.
Row 17: k2tog three times [3 sts].
Row 18: p.
Cut yarn and thread through all sts.

Beak

With 2.75mm (UK 12; US 2) needles and yellow yarn, cast on 8 sts.
Rows 1–6: beg with a k row, work 6 rows in SS.
Row 7: k2tog four times.
Cut yarn and thread through rem 4 sts.

Feet (make 2)

With 2.75mm (UK 12; US 2) needles and orange yarn, cast on 12 sts.
Row 1: k each st tbl.
Rows 2–4: beg with a p row, work 3 rows in SS.
Row 5: k2tog six times [6 sts].
Row 6: p.
Cut yarn and thread through all sts.

Making up

On the body, overlap the side edges of the black piece on to the edges of the white piece and stitch; do the same with the head pieces. Stuff the head with a little polyester fibrefill. Stitch the wing seams, then stitch the wings to the sides of the body. Fold each foot in half and oversew the edges, then stitch them to the base of the body. Pull up the yarn end on the beak, fold the edges into the centre and oversew to form a firm cone shape, then stitch the beak in place in the centre of the face. Sew on the googly eyes.

This cool character will happily keep your egg warm until you are ready to eat it! He measures 12cm (4¾in) high.

Bridegroom

Materials:

3 balls DK yarn (wool or wool blend) – grey,
black and pale peach

small amounts of DK yarn (wool or wool blend)
– white, green, red, bright pink and yellow

polyester fibrefill

button, 3cm (1¼in) diameter

black embroidery thread

2 sew-on googly eyes

1 tiny black button

Needles:

set of four 2.75mm (UK 12; US 2)
double-pointed knitting needles

tapestry needle

embroidery needle

Instructions:

Body, head and top hat (worked in one piece)

With set of four 2.75mm (UK 12; US 2) double-pointed needles and grey DK yarn, cast on 36 sts and distribute between three needles.
Round 1: k each st tbl.
Rounds 2–8: k; cut grey yarn and join in black.
Rounds 9–21: knit a further 13 rounds.
Round 22: (k4, k2tog) six times [30 sts].
Round 23: k.
Round 24: (k3, k2tog) six times [24 sts].
Round 25: k.
Round 26: (k2, k2tog) six times [18 sts].
Round 27: k.
Round 28: (k1, k2tog) six times [12 sts]; cut black yarn and join in white.
Round 29: (k2, k2tog) three times [9 sts].
Round 30: k.
Round 31: (k2, inc1) three times [12 sts]; cut white yarn and join in pale peach.
Round 32: k.
Round 33: (k1, inc1) six times [18 sts].
Round 34: (k2, inc1) six times [24 sts].
Rounds 35–42: knit 8 rounds; cut pale peach yarn and join in black.
Rounds 43–54: knit a further 12 rounds; cast off.

This egg cosy is the perfect adornment for a bridegroom's breakfast table. He is 15cm (6in) high. Pair him with the bride on page 24 to create a happy couple.

Hat crown

Follow instructions for top of the clown's head to round 4, skip rounds 5 and 6, then work rounds 7, 8 and 11.

Hat brim

With two 2.75mm (UK 12; US 2) needles and black DK yarn, cast on 24 sts.
Row 1: (k2, inc1) six times [30 sts].
Row 2: (k3, inc1) six times [36 sts].
Row 3: (k4, inc1) six times [42 sts]; cast off.

Hands (make 2)

With two 2.75mm (UK 12; US 2) needles and pale peach DK yarn, cast on 1 st.
Row 1: inc2 [3 sts].
Row 2: inc1 in each st [6 sts].
Rows 3 and 5: p.
Row 4: inc1 in each st [12 sts].
Rows 6–8: k; cast off.

Sleeves (make 2)

With two 2.75mm (UK 12; US 2) needles and white DK yarn, cast on 13 sts.
Row 1: k each st tbl.
Row 2: p; cut white yarn and join in black.

Rows 3 and 4: k each st tbl.
Row 5: inc1, k to last st, inc1.
Rows 6 and 8: p.
Row 7: k.
Rows 9–12: rep rows 5–8.
Row 13: k1, sl1, k1, psso, k to last 3 sts, k2tog, k1.
Row 14: p.
Rep rows 13 and 14 until 5 sts rem, ending with a p row.
Next row: k1, sl1, k2tog, psso, k1 [3 sts].
Cast off purlwise.

Lapels (make 2)
With two 2.75mm (UK 12; US 2) needles and black DK yarn, cast on 1 st.
Rows 1 and 2: k1.
Row 3: inc1 [2 sts].
Rows 5–6: k.
Row 7: inc1, k1 [3 sts].
Rows 8–10: k.
Row 11: inc1, k2 [4 sts].
Rows 12–14: k.
Row 15: inc1, k3 [5 sts].
Rows 16, 18, 20 and 22: k.
Row 17: cast off 3 sts, k rem st [2 sts].
Row 19: inc1, k1 [3 sts].
Row 21: inc1, k2 [4 sts].
Row 23: inc1, k3 [5 sts].
Knit 9 rows; cast off.

Shirt front
With two 2.75mm (UK 12; US 2) needles and white DK yarn, cast on 7 sts.
Row 1: k.
Rows 2, 4 and 6: p.
Row 3: k2tog, k3, k2tog [5 sts].
Row 5: k2tog, k1, k2tog [3 sts].
Row 7: sl1, k2tog, psso; cut yarn and fasten off.

Flower
With two 2.75mm (UK 12; US 2) needles and bright pink DK yarn, cast on 12 sts.
Row 1: k; cut yarn and thread through all sts.

Bow tie
With two 2.75mm (UK 12; US 2) needles and red DK yarn, cast on 12 sts.
Rows 1–4: k; cast off.

Making up
Stitch the sleeve seams, then stitch the sloping edges of the sleeves to the sides of the body. Stitch the hand seams and insert the hands into the ends of the sleeves. Stitch the shirt front in place. Stitch the cast-off edges of the lapels together then, placing this seam at the centre back of the neck, stitch the lapels in place, overlapping the edges of the shirt front. Add a button where the lapels meet at the front. Bind a short length of yarn around the centre of the bow tie and stitch it in place. Stuff the head and hat with polyester fibrefill. Stitch the short ends of the hat brim together, then stitch the brim in place. Insert a button into the hat crown, pull up the yarn end to enclose it, and stitch the crown to the top of the hat. Stitch the short ends of the flower together and stitch it to the lapel, embroidering a centre with yellow yarn and a stalk with green yarn. Use peach yarn to create a nose and ears, using bullion stitch. Sew the eyes in place and embroider a mouth and eyebrows using black embroidery thread.

Scarecrow
Create a scarecrow using this pattern but with different colours. Omit the hands, using strands of yellow yarn to create straw. Work fewer rows for the hat – 8 rounds instead of 12 – and omit the hat crown, tucking in the top edge of the hat instead.

Wedding Breakfast

Materials:

2 balls DK yarn (wool or wool blend) – ivory and pale peach

1 ball 4-ply yarn (wool or wool blend) – ivory

small amounts of DK yarn (wool or wool blend) – brown, green, bright pink, peach and violet

polyester fibrefill

90cm (35½in) of 12mm (½in) wide sheer ribbon – white

small scrap of lace or tulle fabric – white

sewing thread – white

2 sew-on googly eyes

Needles:

set of four 2.75mm (UK 12; US 2) double-pointed knitting needles

pair of 2.25mm (UK 13; US 1) knitting needles

stitch holder

tapestry needle

sewing needle

Instructions:

Body and head (worked in one piece)

With set of four 2.75mm (UK 12; US 2) double-pointed needles and ivory DK yarn, cast on 36 sts and distribute between three needles.
Round 1: k each st tbl.
Rounds 2–21: k.
Round 22: (k4, k2tog) six times [30 sts].
Rounds 23, 25 and 27: k.
Round 24: (k3, k2tog) six times [24 sts].
Round 26: (k2, k2tog) six times [18 sts].
Round 28: (k1, k2tog) six times [12 sts].
Round 29: (k2, k2tog) three times [9 sts].
Round 30: k.
Round 31: (k2, inc1) three times [12 sts]; cut ivory yarn and join in pale peach.
Round 32: k.
Round 33: (k1, inc1) six times [18 sts].
Round 34: (k2, inc1) six times [24 sts].
Rounds 35–42: knit 8 rounds; cut pale peach yarn and join in brown.
Round 43: (k2, k2tog) six times [18 sts].
Round 44: k.
Round 45: (k1, k2tog) six times [12 sts].
Round 46: k.
Round 47: k2tog six times; cut yarn and thread through rem 6 sts.

Hands and arms (make 2)

With 2.75mm (UK 12; US 2) needles and peach DK yarn, cast on 1 st.
Row 1: inc2 [3 sts].
Rows 2, 4 and 6: p.
Row 3: inc1, k1, inc1 [5 sts].
Row 5: inc1, k3, inc1 [7 sts].
Row 7: k; cut peach yarn.
Row 8: join in ivory DK yarn; inc1 knitwise in each st [14 sts].
Rows 9–20: beg with a k row, work 12 rows in SS.
Row 21: k2tog, k to last 2 sts, k2tog.
Row 22: p2tog, p to last 2 sts, p2tog.
Rows 23 and 24: rep rows 21 and 22.
Row 25: rep row 21 [4 sts].
Row 26: p2tog twice.
Cut yarn and thread through rem 2 sts.

Dress

With 2.25mm (UK 13; US 1) knitting needles and ivory 4-ply yarn, cast on 12 sts.
Row 1: k.
Row 2: k1, (yfwd, sl1 knitwise, k1, psso) five times, k1.
Rows 3–6: k.
Rep rows 2–6 six times; cast off.

Rose (make 2 bright pink, 1 violet)

With two 2.75mm (UK 12; US 2) needles and DK yarn, cast on 12 sts.
Row 1: k; cut yarn and thread through all sts.

Making up

Stitch the sleeve seams, then stitch the arms to the sides of the body. Stuff the head with polyester fibrefill and use brown yarn to create the hairstyle with straight stitches for the fringe; make a bun on top of the head with a knot of yarn. Stitch a piece of lace or tulle fabric to the top of the head, then cut an 18cm (7in) length of sheer ribbon, tie it in a bow and stitch it to the top of the veil. Join the ends of the dress to form a tube. Gather one long edge and pull it up to fit around the bride's body, then stitch it in place. Cut another 18cm (7in) length of sheer ribbon, wrap it around the back of the neck and cross the ends at the waist. Secure it with a few stitches. Cut another 18cm (7in) length of ribbon, tie it into a bow and stitch it to the centre waist. Stitch short ends of each flower together and stitch them to the left hand, adding short lengths of green yarn to form stalks. Cut the remaining ribbon in half, sew a running stitch along one long edge of each piece, pull up the threads to gather and stitch them in place at the ends of the sleeves. Use peach yarn to create a nose and ears, using bullion stitch. Sew the eyes in place and embroider a mouth using bright pink yarn.

The Curate's Egg

For a vicar, follow the instructions for the body and head, sleeves and hands. To make the dog collar, cast on 18 sts, knit 2 rows and cast off. To make the stole, cast on 5 sts in black yarn and work in garter stitch (knit every row) until the strip measures 16cm (6¼in); cast off. Both egg cosies are 11cm (4¼in) high.

Christmas Pudding

Materials:

1 ball DK yarn (wool tweed) – brown

small amounts of DK yarn (wool or wool blend) – green, red and tan

polyester fibrefill

Needles:

set of four 2.75mm (UK 12; US 2) double-pointed knitting needles

tapestry needle

Instructions:

Pudding

With set of four 2.75mm (UK 12; US 2) double-pointed needles and brown tweed DK yarn, cast on 36 sts and distribute between three needles.
Round 1: (k3, inc1) nine times [45 sts].
Round 2: (k4, inc1) nine times [54 sts].
Round 3: k.
Round 4: (k5, inc1) nine times [63 sts].
Rounds 5 and 6: k.
Round 7: (k6, inc1) nine times [72 sts].
Rounds 8–20: k.
Round 21: (k6, k2tog) nine times [63 sts].
Rounds 22 and 23: k.
Round 24: (k5, k2tog) nine times (54 sts).
Round 25: k.
Round 26: (k4, k2tog) nine times [45 sts].
Round 27: (k3, k2tog) nine times [36 sts].
Round 28: (k2, k2tog) nine times [27 sts].
Round 29: (k1, k2tog) nine times [18 sts].
Round 30: k2tog nine times [9 sts]; cast off.

Liner

With set of four 2.75mm (UK 12; US 2) double-pointed needles and brown yarn, cast on 36 sts and distribute between three needles.
Round 1: k each st tbl.
Rounds 2–21: k.
Round 22: (k4, k2tog) six times [30 sts].
Round 23: k.
Round 24: (k3, k2tog) six times [24 sts].
Round 25: k.
Round 26: (k2, k2tog) six times [18 sts].
Round 27: k.
Round 28: (k1, k2tog) six times [12 sts].
Round 29: k2tog six times; cut yarn and thread through rem 6 sts.

Holly leaf (make 3)

With two 2.75mm (UK 12; US 2) needles and green DK yarn, cast on 3 sts; cast off 3 sts and slip rem st on to left-hand needle.
Rep from ** to ** six times more; fasten off.

Holly berry (make 3)

With two 2.75mm (UK 12; US 2) needles and red DK yarn, cast on 4 sts.
Beg with a p row, work 6 rows in SS.
Cut yarn, leaving a tail for sewing up, and thread through all sts.

Making up

Stitch the cast-on rows of the pudding and liner together. Insert stuffing into the gap between the pudding and the liner, then close the top of the pudding and secure it to the top of the liner with a few stitches. Embroider short stitches in a random pattern all over the pudding, using red and tan yarns. Stitch the holly leaves to the top of the pudding. Gather the edges of each berry and pull up to form a ball, then stitch in place.

Jack o' Lantern

Follow the instructions for knitting and making up the pudding and liner but using orange DK yarn. To make a stalk, use green DK yarn and pick up and knit 12 sts on the cast-off edge at the top. Knit 1 round. On the 2nd round, (k2, k2tog) three times. Knit 3 rounds on the remaining 9 stitches. Then (k2, inc1) three times and cast off these 12 sts. Cut shapes from black felt for the eyes and mouth and stitch these in place using black thread.

Egg Warmers

Materials:
1 ball self-patterning 4-ply sock yarn

Needles:
pair of 2.25mm (UK 13; US 1) knitting needles

pair of 3.00mm (UK 11; US 2) knitting needles

stitch holder

tapestry needle

Instructions:

Front and back (make 2)
With 2.25mm (UK 13; US 1) knitting needles and self-patterning yarn, cast on 21 sts.
Row 1: (k1, p1) ten times, k1.
Row 2: k1, (k1, p1) nine times, k2.
Rows 3 and 4: rep rows 1 and 2.
Rows 5–18: change to 3.00mm (UK 11; US 2) knitting needles and, beg with a k row, work 14 rows in SS.
Row 19: k1, sl1, k1, psso, k to last 3 sts, k2tog, k1.
Row 20: p.
Rep rows 19 and 20 until 7 sts rem; transfer sts to a holder.

Sleeves (make 2)
With 2.25mm (UK 13; US 1) knitting needles and self-patterning yarn, cast on 13 sts.
Row 1: (k1, p1) six times, k1.
Row 2: k1, (k1, p1) five times, k2.
Rows 3 and 4: rep rows 1 and 2.
Change to 3.00mm (UK 11; US 2) knitting needles.
Row 5: k.
Row 6: p.
Row 7: k1, inc1, k to last 2 sts, inc1, k1 [15 sts].
Rows 8–10: beg with a p row, work 3 rows in SS.
Rows 11–31: rep rows 7–10 until 5 sts rem, ending with a p row.
Row 32: k1, sl1, k2tog, psso, k1 [3 sts]; transfer sts to a holder.
Do not cut yarn after completing 2nd sleeve but use to knit neck.

Neck
Change to 2.25mm (UK 13; US 1) knitting needles and, with RS facing, knit 3 sts across top of sleeve just completed, 7 sts across top of back, 3 sts across first sleeve and 7 sts across front [20 sts].
Work 12 rows in k1, p1 rib; cast off in rib.

Making up
Stitch raglan seams, then sleeve and side seams. Fold the neck over to the right side.

Cosy Sweater

Various types of self-patterning yarn will produce different effects. Knit a set of these delightful cosies for all the family, in yarns to suit their personalities. These sweaters measure 9.5cm (3¾in) tall.

Bobble Hats

Materials:

1 ball self-patterning 4-ply sock yarn

Needles:

pair of 2.25mm (UK 13; US 1) knitting needles

stitch holder

tapestry needle

Instructions:

Hat (worked in one piece)

With set of four 2.25mm (UK 12; US 2) double-pointed needles and self-patterning yarn, cast on 3 sts and distribute between three needles.

Round 1: inc1 in each st [6 sts].

Round 2: k.

Round 3: inc1 in each st [12 sts].

Round 4: k.

Round 5: (k1, inc1) six times [18 sts].

Round 6: (k1, p2) six times.

Round 7: (k1, p1, inc1) six times [24 sts].

Round 8: (k1, p1) twelve times.

Round 9: (k1, p1, k1, inc1) six times [30 sts].

Round 10: (k1, p1, k1, p2) six times.

Round 11: *(k1, p1) twice, inc1*, rep from * to * five times [36 sts].

Round 12: (k1, p1) 18 times.

Rep last round 21 times; cast off in pattern.

Bobble

Wind yarn around two fingers about 25–30 times. Slip off, then tie a spare length of yarn tightly around the bundle and use this to attach the bobble to the centre top of the hat. Cut through the loops and trim the ends to form a neat bobble.

Hats Off

You can produce different effects by using self-patterning yarns in different colourways. Even a single ball of yarn will produce a variety of different hats, depending on which part of the ball of yarn you begin with. These hats are 6.5cm (2½in) high .

31

Owl and the Pussy Cat

Materials:

2 balls DK yarn (wool, wool blend or acrylic) –
orange and yellow

small amounts of DK yarn (wool, wool blend or
acrylic) – white

2 grey buttons

2 sew-on googly eyes

sewing thread

Needles:

pair of 2.75mm (UK 12; US 2) knitting needles

stitch holder

tapestry needle

sewing needle

Instructions:

Back

With 2.75mm (UK 12; US 2) knitting needles and
orange yarn, cast on 18 sts.
Row 1: k each st tbl.
Rows 2–22: beg with a p row, work 21 rows in SS.
Row 23: k1, sl1, k1, psso, k to last 3 sts, k2tog, k1.
Row 24: p.
Row 25: k.
Row 26: p.
Rows 27–30: rep rows 23–26.
Rows 31–34: rep rows 23 and 24 twice.
Row 35: k1, inc1, k to last 2 sts, inc1, k1.
Row 36: p.
Row 37: k1, inc1, k to last 2 sts, inc1, k1.
Row 38: p.
Row 39: k.
Row 40: p.
Row 41: k1, inc1, k to last 2 sts, inc1, k1.
Rows 42–45: rep rows 38–41.
Row 46: p.
Row 47: k6, turn and leave rem sts on a holder.
Row 48: p2tog, p4.
Rows 49, 51, 53 and 55: k.
Row 50: p2tog, p3 [4 sts].
Row 52: p2tog, k2 [3 sts].
Row 54: p2tog, p1 [2 sts].
Row 56: p2tog; cut yarn and fasten off.

Rejoin yarn to sts on holder and cast off centre
6 sts, k to end.
Next row: p4, p2tog tbl [5 sts].
Next row: k.
Next row: p3, p2tog tbl [4 sts].
Next row: k.
Complete to match first side.

Front

With 2.75mm (UK 12; US 2) knitting needles and
yellow yarn, cast on 18 sts.
Row 1: k each st tbl.
Beg with a p row, work 23 rows in SS, then
cast off.

Wings (make 2)

With 2.75mm (UK 12; US 2) knitting needles and
orange yarn, cast on 1 st.
Row 1: inc1 [2 sts].
Row 2: inc1 twice [4 sts].
Row 3 and each odd-numbered row: k.
Row 4: k1, inc1, inc1, k1 [6 sts].
Row 6: k1, inc1, k2, inc1, k1 [8 sts].
Row 8: k1, inc1, k to last 2 sts, inc1, k1.
Rep row 8 twice more [14 sts]; cast off.

Ears (make 2)

With 2.75mm (UK 12; US 2) knitting needles and
orange yarn, cast on 1 st.
Row 1: inc1 [2 sts].
Row 2: inc1, k1 [3 sts].

Rows 3, 5 and 7: k.
Row 4: inc1, k2 [4 sts].
Row 6: inc1, k3 [5 sts].
Row 8: inc1, k4 [6 sts].
Row 9: cast off 4 sts, inc1 in last st on left-hand needle; turn and cast off rem 3 sts.

Eyes (make 2)
With 2.75mm (UK 12; US 2) knitting needles and white yarn, cast on 8 sts.
Row 1: inc1 in every st [16 sts]; cast off.

Beak
With 2.75mm (UK 12; US 2) needles and orange yarn, cast on 8 sts.
Rows 1–6: beg with a k row, work 6 rows in SS.

Row 7: k2tog four times.
Cut yarn and thread through rem 4 sts.

Making up
Fold the head at its narrowest point, overlap the curved edge over the top of the front piece and stitch it in place. Stitch the side seams, incorporating the long (cast-off) edge of each wing as you do so. Stitch the ears in place at the sides of the head, attaching the side edge of each ear to the side seam. Curl each eye around to make a disc and stitch the eyes in place, with the buttons and googly eyes on top. Pull up the yarn end on the beak, fold the edges into the centre and oversew to form a firm cone shape. Stitch the beak in place.

Pussy Cat
For the owl's pussy cat companion, knit the back section, wings and ears in blue-grey and the front in white. Stitch the cast-on edge of each ear to the side seams on the head. Roll up the 'wings' to form paws and stitch them to the sides of the body. Embroider the features using yellow and black yarn for the eyes, nose and mouth, and black thread for the whiskers. These egg cosies each measure 10cm (4in) high.

Robo-cosy

Materials:

1 ball 4-ply yarn – metallic silver

embroidery thread – black

scrap of craft foam, 2mm thick

2 sew-on googly eyes

metal bar with holes

faux gemstone, oval

small scrap of wool felt – black

chenille stick (pipe cleaner)

Needles:

pair of 2.75mm (UK 12; US 2) knitting needles

tapestry needle

sewing needle

Instructions:

Body
With 2.75mm (UK 12; US 2) knitting needles and metallic silver yarn, cast on 36 sts.
Row 1: k each st tbl.
Rows 2–48: k.
Row 49: k2, *k2tog, k4*; rep from * to * to last 4 sts, k2tog, k2 [30 sts].
Row 50: *k1, k2tog*; rep from * to * to end [20 sts].
Row 51: k2tog ten times [10 sts].
Row 52: k2tog five times.
Cut yarn and thread through rem 5 sts.

Head
With 2.75mm (UK 12; US 2) knitting needles and metallic silver yarn, cast on 21 sts.
Row 1: k each st tbl.
Rows 2–15: k.
Row 16: (k1, k2tog) seven times [14 sts].
Row 17: k2tog seven times.
Cut yarn and thread through rem 7 sts.

Arms (make 2)
With 2.75mm (UK 12; US 2) knitting needles and metallic silver yarn, cast on 20 sts.
Row 1: k each st tbl.
Rows 2–5: k.
Cast off.

Making up
Stitch the edges of the body together to make a cylinder. Pull up the yarn on the last row to close the gap, then fasten off. Stitch the edges of the head together to make a cylinder; pull up the yarn on the last row to close the gap, then fasten off. Cut a strip of craft foam the same width as the height of the head, roll it up and insert it into the head to help create a neat cylindrical shape. Stitch the head to the top of the body. Stitch the long edges of the arms together and insert a length of chenille stick into each one; stitch the ends closed then stitch the arms to the top of the body on either side. Stitch the googly eyes and other components in place using black thread.

Eggy Metal

This robot is 11cm (4¼in) high. For a shorter robot, knit 27 rows instead of 47 when making the body. Stitch on square sequins for the eyes and a metal button for a chest piece. Insert shorter lengths of chenille stick into the arms and roll up the excess knitting, stitching it in place to make chunky hands.

Desert Island

Materials:

1 ball DK bouclé yarn (wool, acrylic or blended) – yellow

2 balls DK yarn (wool, acrylic or blended) – brown, green

Needles:

set of four 2.75mm (UK 12; US 2) double-pointed knitting needles

pair of 3.00mm (UK 11; US 2) knitting needles

tapestry needle

Instructions:

Island

With set of four 2.75mm (UK 12; US 2) double-pointed needles and yellow bouclé yarn, cast on 36 sts and distribute between three needles.
Round 1: k each st tbl.
Rounds 2–21: k.
Round 22: (k4, k2tog) six times [30 sts].
Round 23: k.
Round 24: (k3, k2tog) six times [24 sts].
Round 25: k.
Round 26: (k2, k2tog) six times [18 sts].
Round 27: k.
Round 28: (k1, k2tog) six times [12 sts].
Round 29: k2tog six times; cut yarn and thread through rem 6 sts.

Palm leaves (make 4)

With 3.00mm (UK 11; US 2) needles and green DK yarn, cast on 6 sts.
Row 1: p.
Row 2: k.
Row 3: cast off 4 sts purlwise, purl last st [2 sts].
Row 4: k1, inc1, turn and cast on 3 sts [6 sts].
Rep rows 1–4 five times, then rows 1 and 2 once.
Cast off purlwise.

Trunk

With 3.00mm (UK 11; US 2) needles and brown DK yarn, cast on 12 sts.
Rows 1–16: (k1, p1) six times.
Cast off.

Making up

Turn the island inside out so the purl side is outermost. Roll up the trunk tightly and oversew the edge to secure. Stitch one end to the top of the island. Fold each leaf in half and oversew the straight edges together; stitch the base of each leaf to the top of the trunk.

Give your breakfast a tropical twist with this sunny egg cosy. It measures 12cm (4¾in) in height.

A Ghostly Eggsperience

Materials:

1 ball DK yarn (acrylic crêpe) – white

small amount of 4-ply yarn – black

Needles:

set of four 2.75mm (UK 12; US 2) double-
 pointed knitting needles

stitch holder

tapestry needle

Instructions:

With two 2.75mm (UK 12; US 2) double-pointed
needles and white yarn, cast on 3 sts.
Row 1: k3; do not turn but slide sts to other end
of needle.
Rows 2–6: rep row 1 five times.
Row 7: inc1 in each st [6 sts]; divide between
three double-pointed needles.
Rounds 1–3: k.
Round 4: (k1, inc1) three times [9 sts].
Rounds 5–7: k.
Round 8: (k2, inc1) three times [12 sts].
Rounds 9–11: k.
Round 12: (k3, inc1) three times [15 sts].
Rounds 13–15: k.
Round 16: (k4, inc1) three times
[18 sts].
Rounds 17–25: k.
Round 26: (k2, inc1) six times [24 sts].
Round 27: k.
Round 28: (k3, inc1) six times [30 sts].
Round 29: k.
Round 30: (k4, inc1) six times [36 sts].
Rounds 31–54: k.
Round 55: (k5, inc1) six times [42 sts].
Round 56: k.
Round 57: (k6, inc1) six times [48 sts].
Round 58: (k3, inc1) twelve times [60 sts].
Round 59: k; then turn and cast off knitwise.

Arms (make 2)

Starting with a finger, with two 2.75mm (UK 12;
US 2) double-pointed needles and white yarn,
cast on 2 sts.
Row 1: k2; do not turn but slide sts to other end
of needle.
Rep row 1 four times, cut yarn and transfer sts
to a holder.
Make two more fingers in the same way but do
not cut yarn after completing third finger.
Knit across all sts [6 sts]; divide between three
double-pointed needles.
Round 1: inc1 in each st [12 sts].
Rounds 2–10: k; cast off.

Making up

Stitch the arms to the sides of the body. Use
black yarn to embroider the mouth and eyes.

Eggs from Outer Space!

To transform your ghost into a scary alien, cast on 6 stitches using green yarn, divide between three needles, knit 3 rounds then continue from round 4 onwards. To finish, tuck in the first few rows at the top of the head, then embroider a mouth using red yarn and sew on a single plastic googly eye. These fantastic egg cosies are 17cm (6¾in) high.

Magic Potions

Materials:

2 balls tweedy DK yarn (wool or wool blend) –
dark grey and purple

1 ball DK yarn (wool, wool blend or acrylic) –
grey-green

small amount of DK yarn (wool, wool blend or
acrylic) – pale violet

silky embroidery thread – maroon and black

Needles:

set of four 2.75mm (UK 12; US 2) double-
pointed knitting needles

stitch holder

tapestry needle

crewel (embroidery) needle

Instructions:

Hat, head and robe (worked in one piece)

With two 2.75mm (UK 12; US 2) double-pointed
needles and purple yarn, cast on 3 sts.

Rows 1–6: k3; do not turn but slide sts to other
end of needle.
Row 7: inc1 in each st [6 sts]; divide between
three double-pointed needles.
Rounds 1–3: k.
Round 4: (k1, inc1) three times [9 sts].
Rounds 5–7: k.
Round 8: (k2, inc1) three times [12 sts].
Rounds 9–11: k.
Round 12: (k3, inc1) three times [15 sts].
Rounds 13–15: k.
Round 16: (k4, inc1) three times [18 sts];
cut yarn.
Rounds 17–25: join in grey-green yarn and knit
nine rounds.
Round 26: (k1, k2tog) six times [12 sts].
Round 27: (k2, k2tog) three times [9 sts];
cut yarn.
Round 28: rejoin purple yarn and knit 1 round.
Round 29: inc1 in each st [18 sts].
Round 30: (k2, inc1) six times [24 sts].
Round 31: k.
Round 32: (k3, inc1) six times [30 sts].
Round 33: (k4, inc1) six times [36 sts]; turn and
continue on 2 needles.
Row 1: k2, p to last 2 sts, k2.
Row 2: k1, sl1, psso, k to last 3 sts, k2tog, k1.
Rep rows 1 and 2 eleven times [12 sts].
Knit 2 rows, then cast off.

Sleeves (make 2)

With two 2.75mm (UK 12; US 2) needles and
purple yarn, cast on 16 sts.
Row 1: k each st tbl.
Row 2: k.
Row 3: k2tog, k12, k2tog [14 sts].
Rows 4, 6, 8 and 10: p.
Row 5: k2tog, k10, k2tog [12 sts].
Row 7: k2tog, k8, k2tog [10 sts].
Row 9: k2tog, k6, k2tog [8 sts].
Row 11: k.
Rows 12–15: rep rows 10 and 11 twice.
Row 16: p2tog, p4, p2tog [6 sts].
Row 17: k.
Row 18: p2tog, p2, p2tog [4 sts].
Row 19: k.
Row 20: p2tog twice.
Cast off rem 2 sts.

Hat brim

With four 2.75mm (UK 12; US 2) needles and purple yarn, pick up and knit 18 sts around base of hat, dividing sts evenly between three needles.

Round 1: (k2, inc1) six times [24 sts].
Round 2: (k3, inc1) six times [30 sts].
Round 3: (k4, inc1) six times [36 sts].
Round 4: (k5, inc1) six times [42 sts].
Cast off.

Body

With four 2.75mm (UK 12; US 2) double-pointed needles and dark grey yarn, cast on 36 sts and distribute between three needles.

Round 1: k each st tbl.
Rounds 2–13: k.
Round 14: do not cut dark grey yarn but join in pale violet and knit 1 round.
Rounds 15–21: work a further 7 rounds, alternating the colours on each round to form stripes; cut pale violet yarn.
Round 22: (k4, k2tog) six times [30 sts].
Rounds 23, 25 and 27: k.
Round 24: (k3, k2tog) six times [24 sts].
Round 26: (k2, k2tog) six times [18 sts].
Round 28: (k1, k2tog) six times [12 sts].
Round 29: k2tog six times; cut yarn and thread through rem 6 sts.

Collar

With two 2.75mm (UK 12; US 2) needles and purple yarn, cast on 12 sts.

Row 1: k each st tbl.
Row 2: k.
Row 3: inc1, k10, inc1 [14 sts].
Cast off.

Making up

Stuff the head. Stitch the sleeve seams then stitch the sloping edges at the tops of the sleeves to the main part of the robe on either side. Place the robe over the body and stitch it in place. Stitch the cast-off edge of the collar to the neckline and finish with two lengths of yarn tied in a bow at the front. Use grey-green yarn to create a nose, using bullion stitch. For hair, attach long strands of maroon silky thread all round, where the hat brim joins the head. Embroider the eyes and mouth using black thread.

Wizard

Make a friendly wizard following the pattern for the witch, but knitting the hat and robe in blue yarn, the head in peach and the body in pale grey. Use pale grey or white silky thread for his hair and also for his beard and moustache. When stitching the collar in place, stitch the cast-on edge to the neckline. This magical pair each measures 16cm (6¼in) high (including their hats).

Egg Heads

Materials:

2 balls DK yarn (wool, wool blend or acrylic) – white and red

craft foam, 2mm thick

small scrap of wool felt – red

embroidery thread – red and black

Needles:

set of four 2.75mm (UK 12; US 2) double-pointed knitting needles

stitch holder

tapestry needle

crewel (embroidery) needle

Instructions:

Head

With set of four 2.75mm (UK 12; US 2) double-pointed needles and white yarn, cast on 36 sts and distribute between three needles.
Round 1: k each st tbl.
Knit 22 rounds.
Cut white yarn and join in red.
Knit 4 rounds; cast off.

Head crown

With set of four 2.75mm (UK 12; US 2) double-pointed needles and red yarn, cast on 6 sts and distribute between three needles.
Round 1: k each st tbl.
Round 2: inc1 in each st [12 sts].
Round 3: (k1, inc1) six times [18 sts].
Round 4: (k2, inc1) six times [24 sts].
Round 5: (k3, inc1) six times [30 sts].
Round 6: (k4, inc1) six times [36 sts].
Rounds 7 and 8: k.
Round 9: (k4, k2tog) six times [30 sts].
Round 10: (k3, k2tog) six times [24 sts].
Round 11: (k2, k2tog) six times [18 sts]; cut yarn and thread through rem sts.

Ears (make 2)

With two 2.75mm (UK 12; US 2) needles and red yarn, cast on 8 sts.

Row 1: k.
Row 2 and each even-numbered row: p.
Row 3: k1, sl1, k1, psso, k2, k2tog, k1 [6 sts].
Row 5: k1, sl1, psso, k2tog, k1 [4 sts].
Row 7: k1, k2tog, k1 [3 sts].
Row 9: k1, inc1, k1 [4 sts].
Row 11: k1, (inc1) twice, k1 [6 sts].
Row 13: k1, inc1, k2, inc1, k1 [8 sts].
Row 14: p, then turn and cast off.

Nose

With two 2.75mm (UK 12; US 2) needles and red yarn, cast on 6 sts.
Knit 7 rows, cast off and cut yarn, leaving a long tail.

Making up

Cut a circle of foam to fit the top of the head, place it inside the crown, then pull up the yarn to hold it in place. Fasten off, then stitch to the top of the head. Fold the ears in half, oversew the sides, then stitch the straight edge of each ear to the side of the head. For the nose, thread the tail of yarn into a tapestry needle and work a running stitch all round the edges, then pull up and fasten off, forming a neat round shape. Stitch the nose to the centre of the face. Cut the mouth shape from red felt and stitch in place using red embroidery thread. Embroider the eyes and mouth using black thread. Stitch tufts of red yarn to either side of the head.

Frankenstein

To turn the clown into a monster, knit ears and the main part of the head in green yarn, with the top of the head and the crown in black yarn. Make the eyes from white and red felt and embroider scary features – including a scar – using black thread. These egg cosies are 8cm (3¼in) tall.

43

Sunny Seaside Eggs

Materials:

1 ball DK yarn (wool or acrylic) – bright yellow

2 sew-on googly eyes

small amount of DK yarn – black

Needles:

set of four 2.75mm (UK 12; US 2) double-
pointed knitting needles

stitch holder

tapestry needle

Instructions:

With set of four 2.75mm (UK 12; US 2) double-
pointed needles and bright yellow yarn, cast on
3 sts and distribute between three needles.

Round 1: inc1 in each st [6 sts].
Round 2: inc1 in each st [12 sts].
Round 3: k.
Round 4: (k1, inc1) six times [18 sts].
Round 5: k.
Round 6: (k2, inc1) six times [24 sts].
Round 7: (k3, inc1) six times [30 sts].
Round 8: (k4, inc1) six times [36 sts].
Rounds 9–32: k.
Round 33: (k8, inc1) four times [40 sts].
Round 34: k.
Divide for legs.
**Row 1: k5, turn and leave rem sts on a holder.
Rows 2–24: beg with a p row, work 23 rows in
SS (1 row k, 1 row p).
Row 25: k1, sl1, k2tog, psso, k1 [3 sts].
Rows 26–28: beg with a p row, work 3 rows
in SS.
Row 29: sl1, k2tog, psso.
Cut yarn, leaving a tail for sewing up, and
fasten off.
Rejoin yarn to sts on holder.**
Rep from ** to ** until all sts have been worked
and you have made 8 legs.

Making up

Using tails of yarn, stitch the leg seams from
the tip to about halfway up. Weave in all the
yarn ends. Stitch on the eyes and embroider
the mouth using black yarn.

Eggstra Octopus

*The yellow octopus is 7cm (2¾in) high. For an
octopus with a shorter body, follow the pattern
until round 8, then knit 18 rounds (instead of 24)
and continue following the pattern from round 33.*

Leap Frog

Materials:

1 ball Aran yarn (wool or wool blend) – green

small amount of DK yarn (wool or wool blend) – red

2 sew-on googly eyes

polyester fibrefill

Needles:

set of four 3.25mm (UK 10; US 3) double-pointed knitting needles

pair of 2.75mm (UK 12; US 2) double-pointed knitting needles

tapestry needle

Instructions:

With set of four 3.25mm (UK 10; US 3) double-pointed needles and green Aran yarn, cast on 30 sts and distribute evenly between three needles.
Round 1: k each st tbl.
Rounds 2–19: k.
Round 20: (k3, k2tog) six times [24 sts].
Round 21: k.
Round 22: (k2, k2tog) six times [18 sts].
Round 23: (k1, k2tog) six times [12 sts].
Round 24: k2tog six times [6 sts].
Round 25: inc1 in each st [12 sts].
Round 26: (k1, inc1) six times [18 sts].
Round 27: (k2, inc1) six times [24 sts].
Round 28: (k3, inc1) six times [30 sts].
Rounds 29–33: k.
Round 34: (k3, k2tog) six times [24 sts].
Round 35: k.
Round 36: (k2, k2tog) six times [18 sts].
Round 37: (k1, k2tog) six times [12 sts].
Round 38: k2tog six times.
Cut yarn and thread through rem 6 sts.

Eyes (in 1 piece)
With two 3.25mm (UK 10; US 3) double-pointed needles and green yarn, cast on 4 sts.
Row 1: k4; do not turn but slide sts to other end of needle.
Rows 2–20: rep row 1.

Row 21: turn and k2tog twice [2 sts].
Row 22: p.
Row 23: k.
Rows 24–29: rep rows 22 and 23.
Row 30: inc1 in each st [4 sts].
Row 31: as row 1.
Rep last row 19 times, then cast off.

Arms (make 2)
With two 3.25mm (UK 10; US 3) double-pointed needles and green yarn, cast on 3 sts.
Rows 1–21: k3; do not turn but slide sts to other end of needle.
Cast off.

Fingers (make 6)
With two 2.75mm (UK 12; US 2) double-pointed needles and red yarn, cast on 2 sts.
Rows 1–7: k2; do not turn but slide sts to other end of needle.
Cast off.

Making up
Stuff the head with polyester fibrefill then pull up the yarn end and fasten off. Take the yarn down through the centre of the head, pulling to compress the head slightly, then run through the stitches at the neckline and pull up to gather and tighten slightly; fasten off. Roll each end of the eye cord into a tight spiral, working towards the centre and securing with a few stitches. Stitch to the top of the head, then stitch the googly eyes in place. Stitch three fingers to one end of each of the arms, then stitch the arms in place at the sides of the neckline. Use some spare red yarn to embroider a wide mouth in backstitch.

Definitely something to leap out of bed for, this loveable green frog is 11cm (4¼in) high.

Acknowledgements

For many of the projects requiring double knitting (or sports weight) yarn, such as the pig, owl, cat, bride and bridegroom, I used Sublime Cashmere Merino Silk DK; for most of the other projects I used Patons Diploma Gold, which is available in a wide range of colours, in both DK and 4-ply. For the sweaters and hats I used Regia sock yarn. Thank you to everyone who supplied me with yarns. Thanks also to Josh, who helped with the initial design concepts.